JOB HUNTING
PRO

Toby Tuckerman

Copyright © 2020 Toby Tuckerman

be40262a958b86cdd28055fb68da5367387500043a2d4515f01f5c438798ef53

All rights reserved.

This book or any portion thereof may not be reproduced in any form or by any means, without the express written permission of the author, except for the use of brief quotations in a book review.

Purchaser acknowledges that the material contained in this book is a very specific subset of overall skills and approaches considered important during an interview and that the author and publisher make no representation or warranty, explicit or implied, that the information in this book will by itself significantly influence the results of any job interview.

Cover design by petercover

ISBN: 9798617964266

CONTENTS

PREFACE	iv
HOW THIS BOOK WILL HELP YOU GET THE JOB	vii
1 Taking Control of Your Personality	1
2 How To Make Your Resume Irresistible	7
3 Cracking The Hidden Job Market	18
4 Gaining Valuable Knowledge Before The Interview	25
5 Using Your Soft Skills To Ace The Interview	33
6 Analyzing Your Performance	50
7 Dealing With Post-Interview Like A Champ	54
8 Negotiating Your Way Into A Better Salary	60
BONUS The Mentality of A Successful Job Hunter	68
Epilogue	77
ABOUT THE AUTHOR	80

PREFACE

I remember the time when I began my first serious job hunting crusade and ended up getting interviewed for a position that I thought I was not good enough. The job requirements were completely out of my league and every step of the interview process I was waiting to get eliminated. So it came as a shock to me when I finally got offered the job. Even better, I almost fainted when I heard the salary and benefits package I would be getting. It was two times more than my previous job was paying me! My former co-workers used to think I was naive to think that our jobs were valued that much on the market. After experiencing this revelation, my once held beliefs about job hunting had been shattered and since then I have developed an extremely efficient system for always finding the next best job.

And the funniest part about it? I am just an average worker, not some rock star employee. I don't even have a college degree. And I never got a job, because of knowing someone. I accomplished everything by myself. And it wasn't coincidence or luck that got me there, but my dedication to mastering the art of job hunting. I have learned how to convince any company that I am the perfect fit for them.

A lot of people I knew would start coming to me before their job interviews. At one point, I was lecturing my friend about his resume and the type of mindset he needs to bring to an interview when he suddenly stopped me and told me, that he already took two pages of notes. He jokingly said, maybe I should write a book.

I didn't know how to feel about his remark since I always thought being a skilled job hunter is like being street smart. When you're job hunting, theoretical knowledge gets trumped by practical knowledge. Can you write a practical book? I went online to find that out and saw that most job hunting books are actually written by recruiters, people who have no idea what they are doing and at best, their only decision making lies in passing your resume along. Well, what if I wrote a book, someone who has answered thousands of questions, someone who knows what the usual hiring manager thinks? And I wouldn't bother with some kooky 101 questions and answers, but share the core foundational information, that has proven to work for me and since then has made me view job hunting as a skill that can land you the best jobs?

But most importantly, I wrote this book, because I believe the hiring industry will always favor the one who hires. Companies have the privilege of selecting from an endless supply of candidates who are at the mercy of whatever the company decides. Whereas the candidates need to dedicate dozens of their hours for an unpredictable result. Most companies just ghost you and don't even bother giving you feedback if you get rejected. To make things worse, the job hunting industry exists for helping companies, not the candidates. From recruitment agencies to aptitude tests, all of it has contributed to the current landscape of the job-seeking world. I've seen so many online articles about "7 things you shouldn't say during an interview" or "how to act during a job interview" written by inept recruiters, further spreading useless, faceless information. Interviewing has become what schools and universities have done with exams – an artificial way to determine a person's worth. And for these reasons specifically, a lot of people seeking jobs feel anxiety and undervalue themselves, because they do not know how to present themselves. You might think that reading tens of articles about specific questions will improve your chances of getting a new job, but the honest answer is simple – nobody cares about your answer, it's how you answer the question. There is no right or wrong (unless its a technical interview), its actually just a discussion between two parties – you and the employer, to determine how well you can convince them that you need to be hired.

And that is how this book ultimately came to be – to help everyone get better at job interviews, not by memorizing answers created by recruiters, but by giving you critical knowledge needed to get the best odds at landing your new job. One of the intentions of this book is to help you disarm your fear of interviewing and show you, that there is actually nothing special about the act itself - it's just a skill that can be learned like anything else in life. But most importantly, this book will teach you how to become a job hunting pro.

HOW THIS BOOK WILL HELP YOU GET THE JOB

Job hunting process is often a grueling one. You need to send out many resumes, talk with annoying recruiters, go to long interviews and then anxiously wait for further instructions. Some people get so overwhelmed that they usually take the first, and usually, the weakest offer they can get. When trying to figure out how job hunting works, we go online and realize that every piece of information you look for is fragmented and hidden behind paywalls or sponsored content. Even worse, most experts focus their energy on giving you common sense or irrelevant advice.

This book has been designed with a step by step process in mind, walking you through each stage of the job hunt. More importantly, this book will give you leverage over other applicants. While they are busy reading online articles on how to prepare for job interviews, you will be crushing them with your new-found knowledge of job hunting. This is not a 400-page tome with dry sentences, this is a book written by someone, who values simplicity over complexity. In less than 2 hours it takes to read this book, I will drive home everything you need to know how to succeed at job interviews.

Here's what you can expect to learn from this book, and more:

In Chapter One – Taking Control of Your Personality – you'll be able to learn what's keeping you away from getting more job offers in the first place and eliminate these obstacles before starting your job hunting career.

In Chapter Two – How To Make Your Resume Irresistible – you'll learn about the secret tricks that make your resume stand out and increase the response rate by tenfold.

In Chapter Three – Cracking The Hidden Job Market – you'll learn about the alternative ways of finding a new job, instead of relying on the outdated and unpopular online job boards.

In Chapter Four – Gaining Valuable Knowledge Before The Interview – you'll learn how to effectively research your job position, the company, and even the interviewer.

In Chapter Five – Using Your Soft Skills To Ace The Interview – you'll master the art of interviewing here.

In Chapter Six – Analyzing Your Performance – you'll learn an effective method of reviewing your performance.

In Chapter Seven – Dealing With Post-Interview Like A Champ – you'll learn the best ways of dealing with the post-interview process.

In Chapter Eight – Negotiating Your Way Into A Better Salary – you'll come to understand how negotiating works and learn about different strategies needed to boost your potential salary.

In Bonus Chapter – The Mentality of A Successful Job Hunter – you'll learn about the importance of having the right mentality for job hunting.

Work your way through all of these chapters and you'll end up better equipped than the rest of applicants. Not only that, I promise you will come out with an entirely different point of view of how job hunting works. So let's get started!

1 TAKING CONTROL OF YOUR PERSONALITY

Your personality plays an important role in making good first impressions. If you want to separate yourself from the other candidates, you must find a way of unleashing your own personality. There's no faster way to alienate your interviewer, than providing scripted answers. Even worse, if you start acting overly professional and add too many unnecessary pleasantries to your conversations, you end up looking like a person who is dishonest. Even having the right answers won't save you from these mistakes.

Personality, just like everything else in job interviewing, is a trained skill. Most people will tell you to just be yourself when you go to an interview – that is a big no-no. Having a good personality at interviews is like being good at public speaking – to make people listen to you, some traits need to be either amplified or removed completely.

The Importance of Self-Awareness

One of the great ways to become personable is by working on your self-awareness. However, don't decide for yourself, that you think you're self-aware. It's dangerous to think that you know how everyone perceives you when you're looking purely from your own perspective. It's important you find a person you trust and ask them for their honest opinion about you. Gaining an outside perspective of you can reveal many things you've never considered before. Coming to this realization gives you an edge at becoming more personable. It becomes especially apparent to the interviewer that you've spent time self-reflecting about yourself when you're answering vulnerable questions about your past failures and weaknesses. Self-awareness helps your answers look more genuine and more importantly you gain sympathy from the interviewer.

You Can't Escape Labeling

One of the harshest things about doing interviews is that you will end up getting labeled. You might fit the job description requirements, but make a few wrong moves and the interviewer will get a bad impression of you. It's unavoidable and it's in our human nature to put people into boxes, figuratively speaking. Labeling people helps us deal with human complexity. An hour in an interview is not enough for the interviewer. Assumptions will be made. But where there's a will there's a way. If you're willing to accept labeling exists in interviewing, you can instead become the person in the room you want to be. Projecting yourself to be someone who you're not is a difficult topic to unravel and might be breaching some ethical boundaries, but know this – a different version of you exists in the minds of everyone who knows you. It's only more beneficial, to temporarily become someone you want to be in an interview room. Exhuming confidence might not be your thing, but it does wonders at leaving the interviewer impressed. If you need further convincing, take a look at another well-known way people conduct super short interviews with each other. It's called speed dating.

At its core, speed dating is a dumbed-down version of you trying to get a date within a minute. Nowadays, apps like Tinder exist to help mediate speed dating. The drawback of Tinder is that almost all of the decision making goes based on looks. Whereas the conventional way of speed dating is about you getting to meet new people and trying to connect with them instantly. And the catch is that these types of meetings only last for a few minutes. After meeting a number of people, you're left with only choosing one. But in order to win a follow-up date with them (that hopefully lasts more than a few minutes), they must select you too. All this process of decision making is based on just a few minutes of interaction with each other. Think about it – you're left with only a precious minute or two and presumably, you want to charm that person. Whether you like it or not, you will naturally try to show off your best traits to them. Even if some of those traits might not be entirely true. A good example is how in early relationships people laugh at their partner's terrible jokes. More often than not, it's a sign they want to prove they have a good sense of humor when in reality they probably have a different taste. Some would claim its a dishonest thing to do, but come on, does every relationship start off perfectly genuine?

So whether it's a few minutes of speed-dating or an hour-long interview, both share the same tendency – you will end up getting labeled, based on those first impressions. It's in your best interest to take this into consideration and start showing off your best or conjured traits. Interviewers take well to people who are humble, empathetic, well-spoken, well-read, critical-thinking, self-aware (and more). Take your time and think about any of these traits that you want to showcase. If you've read an interesting book, talking about it can have a good emotional impact on the interviewer. I once had a webcam interview and I purposefully decided to sit in front of a shelf of books. This obviously caught the attention of the interviewer and they asked me to name my favorite book. I was applying for a specialist position and I had some books about it in the webcam's view, but instead, I went with a book about USSR exiles. I explained to them that I wanted to understand such a bleak and horrible part of human history. The interviewer was interested and asked more questions about the book. From our conversation, we both agreed that we take many things in life for granted. I later got a job offer from them. I predicted and seized the opportunity to show off that I am well-read and empathetic, even when in reality, it was the only book I read that year. Still, it's an effective way of leaving the interviewer with a memorable impression of you. Definitely better than being just another plain applicant. Take control of the power to create these short narratives about yourself. Else, you will end up like the majority of candidates – overly pleasant, too professional and worst of all – dry and boring.

Social Media And You

There was once a candidate who used to work as a model, enjoyed posting overpriced coffee pictures on Instagram and had a thing or two to say about politics. The candidate never mentioned anything about any of these things during the interview, because they never got invited. It was part of their digital footprint. And they were being haunted by it. As creepy as it sounds, a lot of companies will conduct a background check on you. Even worse, the interviewer will have formed a premature image of you. Unless your job is being a public figure, I strongly urge you to either disable or delete every social media account you own. Do this at least for the period of job hunting. Use search engines like Google and Bing to see if nothing impressionable about you comes up. To be truthful, depending in which sector you're seeking a job, even having LinkedIn can cause more harm than good. LinkedIn can show with whom you're connected with to other viewers. And it's possible the interviewer will know these people and could start asking them about you. It should be possible to hide your connections from other visitors, so make sure to do that. Always remember, that any information online about you can be used against you, so take control of your privacy and don't let the employer make their assumptions about you.

Conclusion

If you can emotionally engage the interviewer with a good story, you will end up getting remembered. Understanding that self-awareness plays a major role in your interviews is key to coming up with genuine answers. If you're answering your questions in a memorable way the interviewer won't end up thinking you're just another candidate to them. And avoid coming into interviews with a digital footprint behind you. Taking control of your online personality is key to preventing the company from using it against you.

2 HOW TO MAKE YOUR RESUME IRRESISTIBLE

When sending out your resume, you need to keep in mind who will be reading it. A recruiter looks at resumes differently than the internal hiring manager. You're making a huge mistake if you're applying with only a single version of your resume. Not only do you need to anticipate who will be reviewing your resume, but you must also learn how to tailor it to their custom needs. As weird as this might sound, your resume needs to work like the ads you see while surfing the web. Ads are made with the intent to grab your attention. An ad is useless without a clear target audience. If you know who the target audience is, you can apply specific tweaks for your ad and make the ad more successful. In this case, we will be looking at how to apply tweaks in resumes and make them more successful.

Who Are The Resume Reviewers And How To Prepare For Them

The first thing you need to do when looking for a job is by figuring out who is offering it. If you get messaged, for example, on LinkedIn, check if that person is a recruiter. Initially, they will withhold the name of the company the job offer belongs to, but they will be the first ones reading and making a decision about you, based on your resume. And when going through online job boards, check which company has posted the ad. If inside the job description you see the name of the company, but some other company has posted it, you can bet that its most likely a recruitment agency. If not, the next step is for you to Google these companies and figure out whether they are a Fortune 500 company or not. What you end up with are three main types of reviewers who will first assess your resume – a recruitment agency, an internal hiring manager or an applicant tracking system of a Fortune 500 company.

The Cursed ATS System of Fortune 500 Companies

Applicant tracking system or "ATS" has been the bane of job hunting experience since its initial adoption. The reason you've been hearing stories of people never getting answers from big companies is that almost all of them have replaced humans with software as their gatekeepers. Your future depends on an emotionless machine, that makes unknown arbitrary decisions about you. If that's not a sign we're living in dystopian times, I don't know what is. But fret not, there are some ways to fine-tune your resume so you can avoid being eliminated from the selection process.

First of all, and this may sound silly – your resume might not even get read, because of a bad file format. Have you noticed that when you're applying to some companies, they first demand you upload your resume to their website? And then on the next page, you're greeted with a giant application form asking you to retype everything from your resume you just submitted. Now some of those form fields get prefilled, but quite often, they appear empty, as if you've never submitted your resume to them. It gets even more anecdotal if there is no second page that confirms your resume details and the system just eats it up. To minimize the risk of this happening to you, I highly recommend submitting your resume only in .docx (Word) file format. Most of the systems are equipped with dealing with this file format. Use any other format and you're just inviting yourself for more trouble. Even if the website states that you can upload in several different file formats, you should still prioritize sending out Word documents over anything else.

The next important step for your resume is to abandon any fancy graphics you have on it. Anything that is not the text should be removed from the resume. It is true, that once the resume passes the check, a human will eventually review it, but not all ATS systems are equipped with handling images or charts and the problem is that you will not know which one of these systems the company will be using. And just to be extra careful, copy all the text from your resume on a plain-text editor like Notepad and see if any weird symbols pop up – those can potentially trip the ATS and cause further errors. Identify and remove them.

Finally, the most important part of your application – words. One of the annoying things that an ATS does is scanning your resume for words and matching them to the keywords from the job description. Failure to include these keywords results in your application getting rejected. To make things easier, Google for a tool called "resume keyword scanner" to help you with determining which keywords you need to use in your resume. Include these keywords at least a few times on your resume, making sure some of them appear in your job experience tab. People who work in the tech sector like to create a separate skills tab, which is an excellent place for stuffing these keywords if you can't find any other place to mention in your resume.

Machine or Man? No, it's a Recruiter!

The funny thing about recruiters is that they're not that different from ATS. At least if the recruiter is from an outsourced agency. They too will look for keywords and make conclusions without too much critical thinking. These recruiters are motivated to make as many sales as possible – after all, their bonuses depend on it. In fact, some of them will edit your resume to make it more appealing to their clients. You'll notice when talking to them, some of them will give suggestions on what things to study before an interview or straight up give away some answers. They can't make money if they're not delivering new talents. You don't need to use advanced tools like the resume keyword scanners, but you should prepare your resume in a similar manner, making sure to include at least a few of the keywords from the job listing you read from.

The Real Decision Maker – The Hiring Manager

Eventually, after you bypass the gatekeepers, your application ends up with the hiring manager. If there is no recruiter or ATS system to go through, they will perform a similar analysis of your resume, however, they will be laxer and not base everything on keywords. You can bet that a hiring manager is the first one to read your application if you submit it via their website or send it to their company email. If that happens, I highly recommend including a cover letter. It can be as simple as writing it in your email message and attaching the resume (be sure to include two formats, like Word and PDF). Make sure to customize and outline your main motivation why you'd want to work for them. I usually use a cover letter template, that tells a little about myself and the only part of the template I change is when I use a few sentences to describe why I want to work for them.

How I Make My Resume Irresistible

Search the internet and you'll be met with a myriad of generic "tips" on how to make your resume better. They'll never go into clear specifics and leave you hanging when they tell you to "make sure to stand out". Well, here's how my resumes have been working out extremely well.

Use a single-page resume. It's that simple. Unless you're going for an academic position, where you must detail your every accomplishment, there is no better way of delivering your core message than with a limited amount of real estate. Any time your resume spills onto the second page, you now need to cut something out.

You're doing this so that the reviewer can focus on what matters the most. If you have worked for more than one company, always try focusing on one, preferably if it's your current/latest workplace. Craft a small description of what challenges you've had to tackle and what are your accomplishments there. Make sure to integrate keywords from the job description. But most importantly, you need to make sure that either the challenge, the responsibility or the accomplishment sounds important and that you were the main contributor to it. I have met many people who devalue their work and feel irrelevant when trying to apply to new jobs, sticking to some generic descriptions of what they previously worked on. I used to have the same mindset and it messed with my attempts of getting into interviews. There are not enough jobs in the world that are really exciting to talk about, so it's in your best interest if you make them sound exciting. Always respecting the rule of a single-page resume, try to nail down that one thing that you believe will help capture the reader's attention.

I used to be a developer and I had to move pieces of data from one computer to another, ever so slightly changing it little by little. There were several of us doing this. After a week this, even a monkey could do our jobs, it was that dead simple. My colleagues were demotivated about their task and thought they will never get a better job. But when I started job hunting, I was not ready to devalue myself to my new potential employees, so this is what I put into writing -

[Company Name], [Position I Had In The Company]: I developed complex migrations. It was challenging work, as I took the responsibility for integrating our application with legacy systems and solved some problems in unconventional ways."

I made myself the center of attention by putting emphasis on the responsibility part and even thew in a little mystery by mentioning that I used unconventional methods to solve my problems.

And that's the thing when you join any company, you are in this period of onboarding, where you need to adapt to company culture, learn its standard processes and spend time understanding how things are done by the people whom you will be working with. The actual jobs you need to do are usually something you learn over the coming months and quite often you just get stuck with performing the same tasks over and over again. But think about when you're stuck doing the same job and someone else new comes in. They are always full of questions and share an admiration for those who take them under their wing. You were once like that. So even when I tell you the story of how I once did something very boring, it was, in fact, stimulating at first. So try and remember that first excitement you've had and channel it. And as previously mentioned, if a story does not make you the hero of it, then it's not worth telling it.

Getting Feedback

Your resume needs to be reviewed with fresh eyes. Any family members or trusted friends you have, find the courage and show it to them. Even better is showing it to someone who deals with recruitment. Demand their honest opinion. To avoid over-analyzing, make it simple for them and let them sum up in a single sentence, what the first impression they've got from reading it. Then start working from there and ask them what sticks out the most. Your main goal is to accomplish clarity of what you do and who you deem to be so that any person – whether a hiring manager or your family member, can understand it.

Dealing With No Job Experience

Now is the time in your life, where you need to start grasping for straws. Sure, an educational background on a resume is important, but what you really need to aim for, is relating your experience to the job description. You need relevant experience. On your resume, dedicate a special section called "Freelancing and Volunteering" and create a list of bullet points of your accomplishments. Keep two things in mind – how these things relate to what the company is looking for and how to make them sound good. Let's say its an internship position for handling the company's social media account and one of the things you've done in the past was setting up your favorite singer's Facebook page. If you write it as "Made a Facebook fan page for my favorite singer" then it loses its value and becomes trivial. Instead, you'd write it down as "Created a social site for a celebrity, as well as managed content distribution and the regular news channel. The site gained traffic from other several sources". That sounds way better than the former option. It might be more realistic to just say you were posting on the fan page and shared it with other groups on Facebook. But pertaining it to be more professional is what everyone does in any line of work, so technically it's unavoidable. Anytime you mention anything you've done, remember this rule of making it sound more professional and adding some exaggerated value to it.

Lastly, be sure to mention at least a few times how much emphasis you put on teamwork. Anywhere you mention you worked with someone, you better make sure there were words like "synergy, assistance, joint effort, teamwork, etc" in it. The company needs to know that you can play well with others.

Having No Higher Education

It's an age-old fact that higher education gives better advantages. Not only do your odds increase at finding more jobs, but also getting a better salary. One of the recurring requirements lots of companies ask from their candidates is a Bachelors Degree. And to that I say – No worries! Try not to think about it too much and just submit your resume regardless. Negotiations are still possible, and you might still get offered a different position or terms. But if you're looking for a temporary workaround, you might want to consider enrolling yourself in one of the many universities that offer a free online Bachelor's Degree. Many employers will be happy enough to see that you're seeking higher education and it will also help with passing ATS checks. On your resume, just create an entry that you're currently studying for bachelors. When you get asked about your education, make sure to mention the online classes have no conflicting time with the job hours you're seeking. If you end up getting a job, almost no one will ever ask you again about your studies. Whether you decide if you still want to continue pursuing higher education is up to you. Just make sure you're not paying for these classes.

Conclusion

I will not lie – resumes are probably the most headache-inducing experiences you will encounter. Not only do you need to identify who your initial resume reviewer is, but you've also got an important task for creating a narrative about yourself, one that should fit onto a single page. Everyone's biggest concern is what they put on their resume. Most decide to play it safe and just list some dry features or weak buzzwords. Hopefully, from the topics discussed here, it will help you understand, that resumes go through a predictable evaluation process, one which does not favor those who do not understand what they're getting into. After a while of sending resumes out, they become almost superficial for what they stand for and just end up as a way of pleasing the reviewer with what they want to see. If you don't have a lot of job experience, your resume will be used for talking points. Otherwise, it might only be used for a few short questions. Either way, both of these resume scenarios accomplish their job and you've got yourself into the next stage of interviewing. The bottom line is – your resume is not the final word about you, its only purpose is to get people interested in you and in order to stand out from the rest of the candidates, you need to act like a marketer and decide what's eye-catching about you.

3 CRACKING THE HIDDEN JOB MARKET

Finding your new dream job through online job boards isn't the be-all and end-all. In fact, I would argue it's probably one of the least effective methods of job hunting. Without putting yourself out there, companies will only see you as a sequence of data on their computers. If you're not getting enough interview invites through job ads, which is a very realistic outcome, then instead I urge you to check out one of the methods listed below. You'd be surprised how a resume becomes less of a key factor and more of a piece of formality, once you get acquainted with these new methods.

Networking

This is a no-brainer. If you know somebody who works at a company you're interested in applying to, get in touch with them, even if you've only met them once. Never dance around the subject and get straight to the point – even if you barely know them, there's no need for formalities and niceties. Be professional about it and just ask if they could help you out with a referral. A lot of companies operate on referral bonuses, so there is already an incentive for them to help you out.

Social Media

Digging up info about the company, when it comes to the advantages of social media is just the tip of the iceberg. Using social media is actually one of the more powerful ways you can overcome your lack of networking. I sometimes found myself not wanting to go to networking events, because I didn't feel comfortable talking to strangers about job opportunities. And the great thing about platforms like Facebook or LinkedIn is that they eliminate the awkwardness about asking for a job and instead directly connect you with companies who are in need of new recruits.

One of the things I love about LinkedIn is that you can join groups in there. Regardless of your profession, you are very likely to find a LinkedIn group that will connect you with other professionals in your field, employers, recruiters and even discover job postings that you wouldn't find anywhere else. You can try checking out Facebook groups in a similar fashion, although, the key difference between the two is that LinkedIn has an insane amount of recruiters scouting for talent, meaning that any group you join will have an active recruiter in it, who will respond to your job requests.

Besides joining groups, be on the lookout for job ads posted on social media. The cool thing about Twitter is you can browse hashtags like #Jobs or #MarketingJobs or #PRJobs etc. and get in touch with companies via direct messaging or even tweet at them publicly.

Niche Job Boards

Niche job boards are usually more targeted towards a single field or group of people. But they can also offer a different way of finding a job. For example, with the rise of chatbot technology, some start-ups have created intelligent assistants that process your resume and connect you with relevant companies. I've personally used two of these services. They were completely free, took me only a few minutes to fill out some details about myself and a few days later I got in touch with a couple of companies, who didn't even bother asking for my resume.

Meet-Ups

It has become very trendy, especially in the tech sector, to organize meet-ups for professionals. During these meet-ups, key speakers share their stories about their successes and failures. I personally see these meet-ups as a thin veil of employee poaching. Also, quite often these meetups are backed by a single company, that subliminally advertises their in-house products. But that doesn't mean you can't find and connect with people who might just be in need of new hires. And let's not forget that these meetups quite often cost 0$ to enter and have free snacks. Worst case scenario, you end up with a happy belly. Yum!

Company's Website

I've rarely heard from anyone I've met that they've found their job through direct application. A lot of companies share the same sentiment – their job positions on their website are usually outdated by months or even years. More and more companies are outsourcing their recruitment to agencies, while the rest of them just dump their openings on job board websites. Nevertheless, if a company you're interested in has a Careers/Jobs section on their website, you have nothing to lose. Try to get in touch with the company through their specified email or apply directly through one of their job ads on their website. If they have no relevant positions or no positions open at all, you should still write them an email. Do not attach a motivational letter or resume yet. And do not ask if they are hiring in general, without asking for a specific position you're interested in. It's a cold opening, so you don't want to overwhelm them with information yet. Maybe add a single sentence why you've decided to write to them, sort of an extremely short version of a motivational letter. If they don't respond – that's fine. But most of the time, they will respond either with an apology or a promise of getting back to you, once they have a position available. I even had anecdotal evidence of a company responding to my query after more than a few months.

Conferences

A lot of companies like to buy conference tickets for their employees. But what they don't know, is that conferences are literal hunting grounds for new talent.

Most of the companies have hiring managers manning their booths. I know this because I've been doing it myself for quite a few times. I suggest you skip a few presentations (or all, honestly most of them have no value besides boosting the speaker's credibility) and take your time to walk through as many booths as you can. Just come up and introduce yourself to these company representatives, inquire what they do and then ask if they are looking for new hires. Some of these people could end up being your hiring managers, so if you leave a pleasant impression of yourself, they will favor you as the best candidate for the job. Either way, if you end up in an interview, make sure to actively mention in every round, that you've met some of the company's people personally at the conference. Make sure to remember the peoples' names. The more you bridge the gap between yourself and the interviewers through familiarity, the better the chances.

Hackathons

If you've never attended a hackathon before and you're interested to work for a tech company, then this event might just be your ticket to a new job. Hackathons usually last somewhere between 24-72 hours of intense development, where your main goal is to deliver a minimum viable product (MVP) and present it to the judges. Teams of people band together and try to work it out within the specified time frame. It's an exhilarating experience. And hackathons have prizes, but they act more as an eye-candy. Instead of spending money on recruitment agencies, companies like to see what participants are capable of during a live event. Hackathons have become the de facto for finding true talent. Copywriters, Product Managers, Project Managers, Software/Hardware Engineers, Designers, Marketers. These are just a few of the positions that make up the majority of all modern tech solutions. And these are the positions you can easily find yourself invited for an interview. The thing that puts most people off about hackathons, is that in order to deliver something tangible, you need to be able to code. I personally don't think you need to be a coder, just find an idea or project you are passionate about and either join a team or form your own. Make sure to find instructors, who are the employees of the company and chat with them. Ask about the company, the event and then eventually get around to the part where you inquire about their open positions. Senior members, like VPs, will show up as judges during the finale. After the event is over, ask the organizers to provide you with the contact details of one of the judges and write them a personal email. Ask for their feedback on the project you presented. I used to go to a lot of hackathons, from big ones to small ones and I always got invited to job interviews afterward, even when I never won anything. The company would treat you differently, with a sign of respect, because you've shown them your grit. The first round of interviews would become just informal talks and you would get fast-tracked towards the salary negotiation. So it's not about winning the hackathon prizes, but more about winning over the hosts.

Conclusion

You're doing yourself a disservice if you go through the plain old boring job board websites. There are a plethora of other ways to apply yourself for a new position and most of these methods are considered more successful for getting the first interview. To be honest, I think job market websites should be removed from the job search equation. Go online and check out some statistics – the old way of job search is dying. It doesn't mean they are a complete waste of time, but if you're looking to get more out of your time and energy, using something like LinkedIn groups becomes more productive, than just submitting your resume into the void of a job board website.

4 GAINING VALUABLE KNOWLEDGE BEFORE THE INTERVIEW

"If you know the enemy and know yourself, you need not fear the result of a hundred battles. If you know yourself but not the enemy, for every victory gained you will also suffer a defeat. If you know neither the enemy nor yourself, you will succumb in every battle."
— Sun Tzu, The Art of War

There's no better way to shoot yourself into the foot than by going into an interview without researching the company. You don't want to be in a situation, where you struggle with their questioning about your motivation. You need to even out the odds as much as possible and gain enough insight about the company, so you can either use that knowledge for new talking points or have a good speech prepared for your motivation. In other words – you need to convince them that you're not just looking to get payed. It's obvious that money is the main motivational factor, but if you can't bother to do even the bare minimum research on the company, then it speaks volumes about your desperation. Unless you're applying to some obscure company, that has no presence on the internet, it is your obligation to gather as much info about them as possible. In fact, it doesn't always have to be just the company getting researched, but the people who are running it or even the interviewers themselves. You will soon learn that every detail about the company is important and helps further distinguishing yourself from other applicants. Here are some ways I personally have benefited.

Re-Examining The Job Listing

Before going to an interview, I like to come back to the job listing and pick out something, that I consider being an interesting talking point. Usually, the person who made the job description are not always good at understanding the position themselves. It's never a bad idea to impress anyone you're talking to, even at the first stage of an interview with people like recruiters. As an example, I once saw in a job listing, that one of the things the company was looking for in their candidate was good humor. It was weird seeing something like that and I thought that maybe the person who wrote it had no idea what the position was about. Either way, I like to joke myself a lot and it piqued my interest to ask them what was that whole thing about having good humor in the job description. It turns out, this recruitment agency specifically wanted to see if the candidates bothered reading the job description carefully. While I was lucky enough to pick something that stands out very clearly from the rest of the description, it's always important to put your focus on the requirements/benefits the company offers and make sure to use some time to discuss it. I know a lot of people like to joke around how unrealistic the requirements are in most job descriptions. While I can agree that to some extent that is true, it's also important to note this leaves you with more talking points to come up with and use them in your conversations.

Company's Website

There are several things you want to find out about the company when looking at their website. First, see if they have any values or mission statement. These statements are usually very vague and are almost always centered around customer service. Try to utilize their motto during an interview. One of the easiest ways of achieving this, especially if you're seeking an entry-level position, is by answering one of those boring questions "Why do you want to work for us?". Take this as a chance to talk about how you personally were able to resonate with their values and/or mission statement. "I learned that your company believes in the X mission statement. I felt I could find myself resonating with it and I couldn't agree more about the X, Y, Z values. I want to work here because I believe our values perfectly align". Obviously, you don't have to believe it yourself. I never did. But it's important to remember that most of the company founders do believe in these values and mentioning to any senior position interviewer can end up being beneficial for you. It might sound cheesy and fake, but it's better to show that the company is not just another salary machine for you.

Next, you want to learn about the structure of the company and remember at least a few names of the top people. This is usually CEO and few other C-level officers like Chief of Operations. Digging up some info about them, especially the CEO can have a dramatic effect on making a good impression. This is always relevant to know, no matter what position you're applying to. Because ultimately you are working for these top people. Make sure to show the interviewer, that you've made an effort at figuring out how the company is structured and that you're interested to find out at which part of the organization you would be working at.

Finally, some companies maintain a news channel, where they like to share their success stories. Most of these stories revolve around them either getting funded, posting revenue reports or bragging about their philanthropy. You can capitalize on these stories as your motivation to work for them. If the interview has multiple stages, try communicating this to people who are nearest the top of the hierarchy. I like using their success stories as a way of answering what I know about them. There was this time when I was applying to a real estate corporation. On their website, they published their quarterly reports in the current market. They were one of the largest players out there. I had a late-stage interview with one of the senior officers and they wanted to learn about my motives. I told them that I was motivated to work for somebody who owned a major market share of real estate sales. I believed that the company was innovative and ahead of the game, by being able to stay at the top. I wanted to show them I was eager to work and gain experience from someone who knows what they're doing. The officers were happy to hear and commended me for doing my homework. I took their achievements and used them to stroke their ego. Win-win for both of us, as I later got an offer to come work for them.

Doing A Background Check On The Interviewers

Sometimes, you will know in advance who will be interviewing you. If you get the interviewer's full name, make sure to do a background check on them. These people are the ones who have the most power to decide, convince and ultimately help you with getting a job offer. It's in your best interest to use anything you learn about them as an advantage.

Your main goal is to find common ground to sympathize with them. Obviously, you should tread carefully around the interviewer's personal details and never let them realize you've done your research on them. Some might take it well, but most won't. Instead, try to see if you and the interviewer have anything in common and then when the time comes to talk about yourself, you can use one of the things you know about the interviewer as a talking point about yourself instead. As an example, I once researched that the interviewer used to work for a small startup, before moving on in their career and end up working for big corporations. It just so happened, that I also used to work for a startup at the time and I was interviewing for a big corporation, so I told the interviewer that I was looking for a change of pace and wanted to apply myself in a more controlled, less chaotic environment. The interviewer was pleased to hear that.

Another good thing when finding out about the interviewer is to see if they've done any public appearances, such as giving a talk at a conference. It has become the norm for companies to collaborate together and gather in common meeting grounds as industry experts. I remember how I took one of the interviewers by surprise when I mentioned that I saw them online give a presentation at a conference. I specifically made sure to even dig deeper and bring out an example of what I liked about their talk.

Lastly, the most crucial part for you is to find out about the interviewer's position and experience in the company. Knowing this will help prepare for the depth of conversation. If they are a high-level person, they won't be asking you low-level questions and vice versa. You will also come to understand what kind of interview to expect. For example, there are interviews with several stages and if you see that the interview will be with someone who is head of the department, its almost guaranteed you will only get asked very broad questions. Knowing this in advance, you will be better prepared, especially if you have trouble dealing with these types of questions.

The Rest – Social Media, Review Sites, Google, etc.

Take your time and go through major social media outlets like Facebook, Twitter, Instagram, etc. and assess if there is anything worthy of notice. It has become common practice for companies to post their job ads in places like Facebook, so it might be a good opportunity to see if anyone leaves relevant comments about the job. If a company has a blog, read everything they've posted for the past six months. Social media info, in my opinion, is mostly used to see what public image the company is trying to portray. Why would that matter, you ask? Well, for one, a company that has a bad public image is a sign for you to not work there, especially if their reputation gets tarnished by their own employees.

Websites like Glassdoor.com can be useful for not only figuring out the company's work culture but to also learn about the most common interview questions that get asked. Along with this website and many others, they are equipped with crowdsourced information about salary ranges. Besides social media feed and review sites, you want to see what public opinion this company has. I saw one company had issues with its data compliance and several media outlets reported it negatively. It just so happened to be, that later in an interview I was told I would get to work in a department that would deal with compliance. This was a killer opportunity to ask them about their compliance issues and learn how they were dealing with it. We've had a good conversation about it and they were happy in the end that I showed so much interest in them.

Conclusion

Isn't it amazing how much data can be gathered and how wonderfully it pays off, once you use that data correctly? Yeah, this is why Google and Facebook are one of the richest companies in the world – data is the new oil. They have created many new opportunities for finding out more about your potential employer. I sometimes can't believe how things have become so easy for job hunters when websites like LinkedIn came into the picture. If I want to figure out company structure, what projects people are working on and so on, all I need to do is input the company name in the search bar and just browse at my own leisure. People themselves have decided to publicly state, in great detail, what work they do inside those companies. If you have trouble coming up with your own buzzwords or ways to sell, just take a look at those people and use them for inspiration. Other than that, soaking up as much info about the company as possible creates powerful new opportunities to talk about during the interview.

5 USING YOUR SOFT SKILLS TO ACE THE INTERVIEW

(Definition) Soft skills - personal attributes that enable someone to interact effectively and harmoniously with other people.

You can't escape a job interview without a good old fashioned assessment of a candidate's soft skills. Unlike many would like to believe, soft skills assessment does not have a starting or ending point. Any time you talk, you will be assessed. There's a reason why I started this chapter with its definition.

See, the thing about soft skills is that not a lot of people are aware of its origins. It was actually invented by the US Army at the end of the 1960s. The military had become very good at training troops on how to operate machines to do their job. However, more and more conclusions were made, that a group of soldiers are only as effective as how the group was led. So a decision was made to develop a method of capturing how these soldiers were able to acquire skills, that have nothing to do with the machines they were taught to use. At the time, the people conducting research thought, since machines were physically hard to operate, anything besides them was soft to the touch. From those observations, they coined the terms 'soft' and 'hard'. They then went on a full-blown research project at trying to map out if a skill is either soft or hard. I'll spare you the details and just tell you that their findings were met with a lukewarm reaction.

Why am I telling you all of this? Because a military-funded project struggled to make soft skills tangible. They literally spent a great sum of resources deliberating whether reading a map is considered a soft or hard skill. Now think about the interviewers who will assess your soft skills. After decades have passed, is it fair to assume people have evolved and are now capable to effectively perform soft skill checks? We're talking about something that once took an entire project and hundreds of man-hours to do without clear conclusions. No, I think not.

But the times have changed and the hiring sector has decided they know the exact soft skills definition and can even tell you which of them are most valuable. Interviewers, especially recruiters, have an exhaustive list of standardized soft skills they look for in their candidates. Teamwork, Communication, Leadership, Critical Thinking, Positive Attitude and so on. Companies like Google even let you know in advance what soft skills they seek the most. How kind of them.

All of this should tell you two things. First, soft skills evaluation will be taken at face value, therefore you may or may not possess them, because an hour or two is not enough to correctly assess a person's soft skills, especially when not seen in practice. Second, because the definition of soft skills has been heavily standardized in the hiring process, we should be able to utilize these definitions as building blocks for our storytelling. If we know that companies value Leadership, there's nothing stopping us from creating a prepared story of our leadership skills. If we combine both of these conclusions together, then we can agree that soft skills assessment is nothing more than just another set of hoops companies have created for the candidate to jump through. In fact, you will develop an act of showcasing the list of soft skills that you may or may not possess. This is the bizarre reality, one which has been heavily influenced by the hiring sector. And the results are speaking for themselves, a lot of companies have started dropping soft skill assessments and started turning to alternative methods. But, these companies are usually small and in the tech sector, where hiring and headhunting eat up their operating costs.

Ok, so let's say we agree that the ability for the interviewer to correctly evaluate soft skills is not possible. Even worse, interviewers often judge soft skills based on themselves. The candidate is left with no other choice than to influence the interviewer by explicitly telling them what soft skills they possess.

So let's explore in what ways can go on about achieving this.

Taking Control of Your Confidence

Confidence plays a key role in how the interviewer will perceive you. And I am not talking about the kind of confidence where you make boastful claims and answer every question with pride. I am talking about the type of confidence, where your answers make sense to you.

Because, if you can believe what you're saying, then surely the interviewer will believe it too.

Some of the main symptoms of low confidence are as follows:

Your answers are unoriginal (i.e. you Googled them)
Your answers are trying to please the interviewer
Your answers sound doubtful

One of the antidotes for these symptoms is for you to act knowledgeable. It's not easy to answer every question in a well-informed manner, but there is one technique you could try. You do this by looking back on your life and fishing for clear examples when you got into a situation where you were able to dominate a conversation with your knowledge and facts. At that moment, you were determined and believed what you were saying was 100% true. The next thing you need to do is encapsulate those feelings that you were experiencing. This is the state of mind you want to take control of. However, not everything is perfect and you need to hone it a little more. You need to identify if your answers hold any negative feelings in them – you must get rid of them. No sarcasm or indignity allowed. You'd be surprised how many people I've seen in interviews using their sarcasm as a form of confidence – it didn't work out for them and they just ended up looking unsympathetic.

If you can't think of the time you showed off your confidence, you can try simulating it by answering something that sounds absurdly obvious. Can pigs fly? No. Why? Because they can't. But why? (Sometimes the interviewer will challenge you even further). Pigs do not have wings, therefore they can't fly. As absurd as the example is, you end up using this emotional experiment as a building block for creating a more confident version of yourself.

The second thing you need to do is beat up your Impostor's Syndrome. I have battled it and still have trouble with it to this day. A lot of people will tell you, that this is what humble people feel. Well, from my experience, this has only caused me a lot of anxiety and gave serious blockage during my career. It's a nice syndrome to carry around when you're just starting your first job, but it only becomes a burden when you want to start advancing in your career. You should never stop learning, but you should also adopt the thinking, that nothing can be accomplished by just learning. Action breeds more action. That means sometimes you will not have enough experience and you will need to learn as you go. And those actions will often be failures, but that's the process of becoming distinguished and experienced. Truth be told, a lot of companies are willing to take the risk if you're willing to show you're able to improvise as you go.

And if you still haven't noticed, job ads are usually bloated with requirements. There is nothing more dreadful when you get invited to an interview and you remind yourself of the job requirements you read from the ad. Do not get bothered by that. You're already talking to them, which means they see something in you and the only thing you need to be thinking about is how to convince the company you are the right fit. This is it. So when you're in that room, you should not dwell on what skills you're lacking. Instead, you need to tell them stories of how you either use your current skills or how you came to possess them.

Lastly, things might not always come off perfectly

and you will need to learn how to shrug it off. Failure is part of success. If you botched up the interview, don't just think negatively about it – instead, think of ways you can learn from your mistakes.

When I first signed up for boxing lessons, it took me a great deal to actually learn how to punch and move. I would always keep second-guessing myself and keep seeking comfort from my coach. Far too many times, I would ask him whether I am doing it correctly or not. I sort of started to annoy him and one day he told me, that if I don't start throwing my punches with confidence, then I will never get out of the fundamentals. Yes, he was there to assist me at all times and he showed me dozens of times how to properly throw a punch. And yet I still kept stumbling. So how did I finally learn to throw a punch? I gambled and just started doing my best instead. After some attempts, I would no longer second guess myself. If I failed, I owned up to it, learned from my past mistakes and attempted another try.

As a matter of fact, the more interviewing you will do, the more confident you will become eventually. It's inevitable. The process of hiring is formulaic and interviewing has become a skill. I strongly urge you to go to as many interviews as you can. If you are eyeing a job you really want to get hired for, first go to other interviews, so you can build up your confidence. Eventually, your confidence will empower you so much, that even the cookie-cutter answers from the internet will convince the interviewer.

The Power of Eye Contact

This might come as a surprise to you, but some time

ago, I had a problem maintaining eye contact with people. Some of the first job interviews I went to, I didn't realize what leverage eye contact could create for me and I would instead resort to finding a specific corner of the room and just fixating my gaze onto it. Only after getting an interview with a company I really wanted to work for, I decided I really needed to up my game and present the best version of myself. Just talking wouldn't be enough and so I took it upon myself to learn the art of convincing people. Being nervous about something I had never done before, I did a lot of research. Eye contact came up as the most referenced way for convincing people. In fact, just about any important interaction in life requires you to maintain solid eye contact. Sometimes, a thought process or a feeling can be better expressed by just looking into someone's eyes. Your words become more memorable. You become more memorable – people will take notice of you. There are also studies that show, how people are more likely to trust you. Basically, you're missing out on a whole lot, if you do not use any sort of eye contact. And the best thing about it – its most effective when used subtly. You don't actually have to stare into someone's eyes the whole conversation. After I came to this realization, I developed my own system. Because of having an issue with maintaining my own eye contact with people, I had no problem using it sparingly. So, for asking questions and listening to the interviewer it's considered important that is obvious enough. But that leaves out answering questions. Here's when a deficit of eye contact becomes most powerful. I start by answering the question without looking at the interviewer's eyes. Only when I am nearing the end of my answer, I then return my gaze back at the interviewer. Recently published studies have delved deeper into the topic of eye contact and the technique I am describing here, shares some commonalities with those studies. Basically, if you can keep the person engaged via your eye contact with an on and off basis, you leave them with a powerful cognitive engagement. Your answers sound more powerful when you are able to anticipate seconds before you're about to finish. These answers need to contain "the drop". A drop or beat drop in popular music, especially electronic dance music styles, is a point in a music track where a sudden change of rhythm or bass line occurs, which typically is preceded by a build section and break. So your "rhythm" of when you're speaking needs to be amplified with a drop – in this case, when you gaze back into the interviewer's eyes. When you get handed a question you easily know the answer for, you can start the buildup by putting on a thinking face and looking elsewhere in the room. Only when you're nearing the end, your eyes need to dart back at the interviewer and you can then deliver a powerful last sentence.

Don't Forget Your Body Language

You want to sit straight in your chair, hands on the table. When you're talking, try to sometimes use your hands with palms out. You want to look as open to them as possible. Arms crossed, slumped in the chair, hands under the table – some of these might distract the person you're talking to or leave them with a negative impression of you. When an interviewer speaks, you can use your hand to hold under your chin. Also known as the Thinking Statue pose, you show the interviewer that you are engaged in the conversation by actively thinking about what they're saying. Sometimes nodding, just to confirm you are listening or saying "aha" also helps. Try to not overuse it though, as it can just start to annoy the person talking to you. Also, hand gestures, do not forget to use them. They help us take what's on our mind and make it intelligible to others. They will power up your thinking, create clearer thoughts and you will be able to speak in simpler sentences.

Dealing with the three most common question types

There are hundreds of different questions you might get asked during a job interview, but almost all of them boil down to just three types, minus the technical ones. Since this book is not aimed at any particular job, I will leave out the technical questions and focus on the three categories, which are:

How you interact with coworkers
How you communicate with your manager
What motivates you

Before I go over each of them separately, you need to understand, that we are not here to focus on the specific type of questions from these categories. The answers themselves never matter if you can't first understand the fundamentals of why you are getting asked these questions. A most common mistake lots of newbie job hunters do, is they go online and look up top interview questions and answers. Recruiters and hiring managers will see you through immediately if you resort to cookie-cutter answers. This is why its way more effective to just tackle the bigger issue itself and learn more about the methodology of why you're getting asked these questions and how you can react to them.

How You Interact With Coworkers

Here, the interviewer is trying to find out if you are able to work with other people. Anytime you get asked about how you would handle conflicts, how to work with teammates or how to handle criticism, you first need to stop and think about the person you most care about – the hardships and experience you had with them can be applied to a certain degree with a colleague. Think about that relationship and ignite the empathy within you. All and every question regarding team culture or colleagues, none of them should go answered without empathy involved. And if that isn't clear enough, then you want to present yourself as a caring, selfless, encouraging and inspiring person to everyone. The whole idea behind a company is making humans work together and achieving results collectively. That could not get more obvious. In own my experience, lots of teams usually have a person whom I call a "pillar" - someone who motivates and holds the team together. Quite often, once the person leaves that team, shortly after a lot of others follow suit. It is these "pillars", especially for establishing new teams, that employers are looking for. And it never hurts to have more than one. I've seen people with mediocre job skills get accepted, only because they are so motivating and feel good to be around with. In fact, I recall when I talked with a former colleague of mine, who was on his 2nd job in his career and didn't have much going for his resume, but wrote in it, that he plays basketball and strongly motivates others around him to do their best. It was a position in a corporate office environment applying mathematical knowledge. And yet the interviewers actually stopped and asked him more to elaborate on his motivational skills. Later, they would call him back and congratulate him on getting the position and mention that they were impressed and eager to get someone who could bring enthusiasm to their team. After all, working in a corporate environment and crunching big numbers can definitely suck up the morale after a while. Showing that you care for your team is what matters the most in the end. Think about it – you are already applying to a job that you can do, so you really need to focus on how to emphasize yourself as the perfect team-player.

All in all, this category of questions I would consider to be the easiest. There really is no other way to answer them, then being a decent human being. No aggression, no negative feelings or any sort of sarcasm should be shown. Only empathy and compassion. Following this simple rule will get you through any of the questions. Do not overthink these questions when you get asked. Worst case scenario, if you cannot think of an answer, just roll with the easiest answer there is - "I would ask HR". This at least shows that you know where to direct your queries in difficult situations.

How You Communicate With Your Manager

If you're applying for a job position that has no managerial responsibilities, then all you need to do is show your understanding of how management works. When you get questions on how to handle a situation with your manager, you should always answer by first talking to your immediate manager and only then, if a conclusion cannot be reached, you would involve HR or superior manager who is in charge of your manager. In no situation should you ever involve your colleagues when you have a dispute with your manager. This is a red flag for more escalations to be handled inside the company and further disturbances to be caused (such as rumors, loss of morale, etc.). You need to show the interviewer that you respect the chain of authority and know-how to report and resolve issues with management. You also should show the interviewer, that you understand your manager's duties, such as receiving constructive performance feedback. One of the key responsibilities a manager is entrusted with is to provide growth for their subordinates. Think of a single example of how you got feedback from your manager and how you utilized it to grow as a professional. The relationship with your manager is like a cycle. You do your job and then review your performance together. Rinse and repeat. You never need to occupy yourself with anything that does not involve doing your job (in theory). Any edge case scenarios where something happens negatively with the manager rarely gets resolved professionally. If you get thrown one of the "what if" scenarios of some moral dilemma, then again, you never take action in these scenarios, before you go over with your manager first, even if they're the source of the problem. Talking first, actions later. This way you prove the interviewer that you will not act as a hotheaded person and instead resolve disputes professionally.

Sometimes you will get asked about leadership questions. Big corporations like to include leadership and managerial questions, but only as a form of a metric about you. You will most likely not get offered a manager's position, especially if it's not something that has been discussed prior to the interview. If you get these questions, just remind yourself, that this quizzing will not determine if you get the job or not. It will only be used for the mere purpose of collecting more data about you.

What Motivates You

"Why do you want to work for us?", "What are you working on right now?", "What are your expectations?"... By asking these questions, the interviewer tries to uncover your motivation, goals, and intentions. They can also, without even conducting a technical interview, determine your professional prowess. And sadly, this is where a lot of candidates will fail. You need to truly amp up your marketing skills and show off why you are such an important asset to your new prospective employer.

Here are two things you will need to work on in order to become great at answering these questions: practice your storytelling and include "I" often in these stories. I did this. I did that. The formula for constructing such stories follows this: pick a challenge or problem you've experienced and have a good understanding of the whole situation. Make yourself the center of it. Mention your involvement cooperating with teammates, but be explicit that you were the catalyst of the story. Now try to get this story under a minute or two. Add excitement in some parts of the story. And there you have it. You usually construct such stories about the work challenges you had. If they straight up ask you about challenging tasks, you can add more complications to the story, to make it sound more difficult. And remember – you are the hero/heroine of this story. I've had people tell me exciting stories, only to forget to add themselves in there. 'That's great! But what was your part in this?' That's one of the most dreadful questions you should avoid getting asked. The person who listens to you needs to understand all the achievements and failures you've had during that storytime. No matter how mundane your work looks to you, you need to extract the most exciting parts from your past experience and create at least one story out of it.

You also need to convince them that you are motivated for the job. Not having a clear reason why you want to work with a company is a red flag for them to not hire you. Especially if they need to spend resources onboarding you, they can't take risks and need to be convinced you want to work for them. I've found there are a few good ways to tackle questions when asked about your motivation. First is to actively show your motivation during the interview by asking them a series of organizational questions, and then homing in on the follow-up questions. Ask about organizational structure, what department you're applying to, what current projects, vendors or companies they collaborate with. Ask what functions or processes they use in their day to day business. Basically, you need to look like a person who is trying to get the big picture of the company. That already shows them you are curious about their work environment and that you aren't here strictly looking for a better salary/benefits. Obviously, showing off active listening skills and adding excitement helps too. Asking about company culture is also a great way to show that you care with whom you work with. In reality, most of the company cultures are the same, but middle management and hiring companies really try to put emphasis, especially for a younger generation of workers, that they have a great company culture vibe. If you are interested in that culture, you show that you are motivated to work for that company. You'd be surprised how a lot of candidates get rejected because they are not 'culturally fit'. I like to think that a company is like a country. It has its own culture, politics, and people. Joining a company is like becoming a citizen. And if you want to succeed in such a country, you must show your patriotism and engagement. No hermits allowed in these countries. Avoid being the hermit in this situation and show your interest in what this country does.

This last part deals with flattery. Let's be honest – almost every company is a faceless entity and you never actually know what's happening inside of it, until you join it. Sure, some well-known tech companies like Google like to market their work opportunities where they literally have a giant campus, but what do the rest of them offer? Nothing, maybe besides a bigger salary and a change of environment. If you're young and motivated, you might have some naive ways of saying why you want to work for them, but the professional way of flattery is by talking about the domain model the company works with and how it fascinates you. If you are unfamiliar with what a domain model is, it's basically what services the company offers. Like leasing houses, being a review website or offering gardening e-services and so on. Time and time again, I saw that the most perfect ways of flattery were by gushing about their domain. I actually had to wise up on a specific Scandinavian mortgage model before going to an interview. I impressed them that I did my homework. In hindsight, after working there for a few months, I realized I was totally talking out of my ass during that interview, but I guess I flattered them by bothering to even comprehend their domain model from the beginning. This is a killer deal for anyone who wants to hire a new candidate – if they show strong interest in their domain, they not only get flattered but also know you are motivated. Two birds with one stone. Also, try finding public videos of the company giving talks in conferences so you can show them you've shown interest in their produced content.

Conclusion

You should now have a solid grasp of how you can react and interact with the interviewer. Even though the hiring sector has complicated the soft skill interview process immensely the core principles still remain the same – use your body language and focus on solving the underlying concerns the employer has about you. They want to know how well you function as a team member. They also need to be assured you can get along well with management. But most importantly – you need to drill your motivation into their heads.

6 ANALYZING YOUR PERFORMANCE

After the interview is over, I personally feel physically and emotionally drained. After all, it takes a lot of physical and mental preparation to show off and sell yourself to others. And just like when you're done after the exams, it feels as if a huge weight has been lifted off of your chest. During this time, it's extremely important to find the nearest place to sit down after the interview and recollect everything that had just happened. The most annoying thing I find about interviewing myself is that you get overwhelmed with a ton of info about the company, how it operates, what it wants from you, what they offer and tons of other minor details. The last thing you want to happen is half-remembering stuff about the interview. Even worse, you also need to recall what you've said to the interviewer. Sometimes I mention things I wouldn't to other companies, things like little white lies or stories that are personalized towards the company itself. It will happen, during the heat of the moment. This becomes even more crucial when you're actively going to not one but several different interviews, needing to keep tabs on things that have been promised or discussed over.

So take your time and write down as much as you can. Pour your thoughts, do not try to filter them yet and jot down as much stuff as you can remember from the conversation you've had. Then read it over and clean it up. With the thoughts now recollected, you can use this information as a way of remembering necessary details about the job before any other follow up interviews, have stronger insight for salary negotiations and even cross-compare with other interviews you've had. In fact, I have prepared a cheat sheet that I have been using myself and found to be very useful at picking things that I consider most important to remember about.

Copy Of Job Description (if there is any) – just a link to the job ad I got invited over to talk about. As previously discussed in the book, sometimes you need to beat the ATS and decorate your resume with the keywords that you aren't necessarily dealing with. So just re-reading the job ad before every stage of the interview helps out.

Resume – since it never benefits you to send out the same resume to different companies, you need to keep track of which resume has been submitted to each company.

Preparation – what sort of research I have done about the company and the position, before the interview.

Log – this is where you should just put down as much stuff as you can remember about the interview. You can, later on, create your own additional bullet points and organize these thoughts more thoroughly.

Soft Skills Test – Any questions that stood out from the interview, especially the ones that you feel you've struggled with, write them down here.

Technical Skills Test – If you were given a task to solve, recall as many details as possible, as the task might be used in follow up interviews as a talking point.

Position And Responsibilities – arguably the most important section to fill. What position and responsibilities were advertised on the job ad, how they were actually described by the interviewer and then how you finally concluded it all yourself. This becomes very important at later stages of interviewing. You will need to demonstrate your comprehension of what is being asked of you to do at the company. This will also help out during salary negotiation.

Salary And Benefits - Any salary or benefits that were discussed, goes here. Also include in this part the salary range, if any, that was mentioned by the recruiter or job ad.

What You Learned About The Company - This is where I usually try to form my understanding of how the company operates, which departments are cooperating together and how I believe I would fit into the whole picture.

As well as other important details such as the location of the office, working schedule, when to expect an answer and so on.

Finally, I suggest to grade yourself on how you personally believe the interview went. If you think you bombed somewhere in the interview, identify what might have caused it. You should also try to think of what was so great about you. I've found that I prematurely conclude the success of the interview based on the emotion I had after I was finished with it. This is not ideal when trying to look from a more critical perspective. Early in my career, I would get surprised, where I would think I struggled the entire interview only to find I would get invited back for more. This is why I started keeping track of everything because then I can look at my notes and see what has possibly saved me. Another important thing to do is going back and looking through the notes, so you can prepare a list of questions that concerns your own well-being in the company. The majority of the interviews are usually spent talking mostly about either you. When the interview is about to be over, you might not even be able to formulate your concerns you have about the position or the company, because you are just mentally drained from all of it. So treat this aftermath recording two ways – evaluating yourself and the company.

7 DEALING WITH POST-INTERVIEW LIKE A CHAMP

Once you're done with your interview, the waiting game begins. Always make sure to ask who will be your point of contact and when can you expect an answer from the company. But it doesn't stop there. After all, you will get assessed in more than one round of interviews. Either way, you need to come up with a personalized thank you note, establish your followup strategy and in the worst-case scenario, learn how to deal with rejection.

Crafting The Perfect Thank You Note

Don't be one of those people who write physical handwritten thank you notes. Nor should you text or call the hiring manager. All you need is to write a single paragraph email and send it a day after the interview. Waiting for the next working day is important, especially if you have interviewed on Friday. What I also like to do, is to send the email during the first working hours in the early morning. Most managers' email boxes get filled with morning agendas, so it's better if your letter ends up at the top of the pile.

If you want to stand out, write a personal thank you note. Do not write more than a single paragraph. If you write more, you just end up looking desperate or become more of a pain in the neck. The first sentence is the easiest, as you just blurt out thanks for the interviewer's time. The latter part, however, is up to you on what you want to include in it. Strategically, you have two choices. You can either further establish your expertise by sharing an online resource of the topics you've discussed during an interview and adding your own commentary to it. Or, you can remedy one of the questions you think you've bombed during the interview and come up with a different answer.

Here are two examples:

(Sharing expertise)

> Hi [Name],
> Thank you for meeting up with me. I had a great time talking with you, especially when it came to the subject of the lean-agile discussion we had. I actually attended one of the workshops led by Mr. Rossman, the renowned lean-agile coach. It just so happens that he shared with me and other attendees his latest presentation slides. I have attached a copy of these slides for you. I think you'll find the new insights on the iteration review chapter as thrilling as I did.
> Best Regards,
> [Your Name]

(Recovering yourself from a question you answered poorly)

Hi [Name],

Thank you for meeting up with me. I had a great time talking with you. I also want to take this opportunity and clarify myself regarding the question about the company goals and how I would help achieve them. I admit that my expertise is not the only component for achieving your company goals and I would like to add, that I am currently maintaining a knowledge base for my current company, where employees are using it daily. I believe that knowledge sharing is a very important factor in having successful projects. I hope this brings more clarity to you about myself.

Thanks again,
[Your Name]

Following Up

If you were given by the interviewer a time frame when they would be getting back in touch with you, you should only follow up with them after that mentioned time has passed. Afterward, you need to send out another single paragraph email, this time, just establishing that you are still here, you are still interested in the job and when can you get an answer from them, since the given time had passed and they still didn't get back to you. It's common for companies to ghost you and never write back to you, so if your follow up email doesn't get answered, don't bother writing to them anymore. Luckily for follow-ups, they can be generic, so feel free to use this one as your template:

Hi [Name],
I just wanted to check with you if you're still considering me for the [job position]. I am still very interested in working for your company and the opportunities it offers. I look forward to hearing from you soon.
Best Regards,
[Your Name]

Dealing With Rejection

It's a gut-wrenching feeling when you hear for the first time that you're not the candidate they're looking for. I won't lie, it will be hard on you. But there is a silver lining. They bothered replying to you. You would be surprised how many companies don't bother coming back with an answer. Even better, you can come out on top of it and write them back an email, thanking for their time considering you. Ask to stay in touch with them for future job position openings. Even better, try to connect with them on LinkedIn. I have witnessed many examples myself personally, where someone takes their rejection really well and later on, even as soon as few months have passed, they would get another interview invite. Sometimes, they would skip the interviewing and just go straight for the salary and benefits, because they can still remember everything about you. This has personally happened to two of my former colleagues. I still frequently get job opportunities from several hiring managers that I got rejected by.

Never Stop Hunting

Even if you aced your interview, you should not cease looking for more job opportunities. Your interviewing skills only keep growing after each meeting and your pool of possible job opportunities only further increases.

Conclusion

Having a solid strategy at approaching the post-interview process is as important as the interview itself. Learning to utilize thank you notes, helps you to either recover or improve yourself as the candidate. Follow-ups help you remind the company about yourself. And if you get rejected, learning to keep your chin up and requesting to remain in contact can still create new opportunities for you. More importantly, your patience will be tested. Do not succumb to anxiety and think the worst will happen. Remain optimistic and do not settle down with your job hunting, until you have at least a few offers waiting for you.

8 NEGOTIATING YOUR WAY INTO A BETTER SALARY

Money. It's what has been driving this world to revolve around for ages now. The source of both happiness and frustration. Some people claim money doesn't make you happy. Well, it sure doesn't hurt to have a bigger disposable income – after all, more money means you can take more actions. You can get a better loan, get kids through college, donate to your favorite charities and so on. In fact, I would be lying if I didn't say more money brings more confidence. There is a point, where money becomes redundant and brings its diminishing returns, but it takes a while to end up in that magic bracket. More often than not, you will be told by many, that earning more money means you need to have worked for years. Even worse, a lot of people will at some point learn, that they are only earning half as much their colleagues, even when their work experiences are similar. Queue the explanation, how these colleagues have certifications or some other irrelevant experiences that lets them have more cash in their pockets. I can tell you for a fact that salary doesn't always directly correlate to how experienced you are. I have seen the anecdotal evidence, where someone who has worked 10 years more than me and is many times more experienced than me, ends up earning less than me, working in a position that makes him more senior than me. And it's not because I am some rock star employee. Its the opposite – I was and always have been an average worker. The first four jobs I worked, I always earned similar to what everyone else did. But once you start talking to more confident people and learn what they earn compared to you – well, it just makes you wonder how much better they are than you. In fact, you know their job performance is no different than yours. You might say it's how management values them but that couldn't be further from the truth. The mystery why these people earn more than you has a simple twist – they knew how to negotiate their salary. And in this chapter, I will show you how an average person can go about and end up with the not so average salary.

Why You Should Never Skip The Negotiations

Websites like Salary.com published their findings, where they claim that 62% of the survey participants never bother negotiating their salary. The survey states why job hunters choose not to engage in negotiations for the following reasons: they are afraid of getting rejected, they think they might come off dumb or they believe they will get eliminated from the interview process. In other words – fear of the unknown. And I get it, its a daunting task, especially if you're not currently employed and risk losing a job opportunity. But on the other hand, you will be missing out on probably the only way of getting your salary bumped. It's a widely known and researched topic, that the best way to get a higher salary is by getting a new job. Pay raises inside a company are extremely complicated and at the end of the day, they are seldom satisfying. I have found the best way to improve my negotiation skills by applying to jobs that I am not very excited about. If I am unmotivated to get the job or I don't worry about getting eliminated from the interview process, once the time comes to talk about money, I can state my requirements more calmly and confidently. Sure, it may misfire – it happened to me quite a few times before. I once went to an interview that was happening in an office that hasn't seen a renovation for decades, talked to the hiring manager who came off dishonest and in general, the vibe that I got from all of it didn't sit right with me. So when the time came to discuss my salary, I just gave them a single number, which I thought at the time was reasonable. I didn't get scared when the hiring manager almost laughed it off. I stuck to my guns. After the meeting, I was informed a few hours later that I got eliminated from the interview process because they couldn't hire somebody so expensive. I was totally OK with it because I wanted to see their reaction and work on my negotiating skills. I lost my personal time, but instead, I gained a good amount of insight. I was asked to argue why I believe I should be paid so much, what market value do I believe the job has and so on. Challenging questions, some of which you may or may not get asked, but getting to practice it on an actual hiring manager is an invaluable way of conquering your fear and learning more about negotiations. And to add to the story, I later learned that the people inside that specific company were severely underpaid and the salary I was asking for was actually very reasonable.

Do Not Give Your Preferred Salary Straight Away

Salary negotiations can start as soon as you receive your first phone call screening. My favorite method of deflecting this question is by stating that I first want to figure out the responsibilities, benefits and growth opportunities that the job offers before I can come back with my preferred salary requirement. This doesn't work well with recruiters, because they are required by their clients (the company you are interviewing for) that each candidate agrees to come with an already formed expectation of the potential salary. You can instead try asking the recruiter what potential salary you can expect from the company. Most recruiters work like conveyor belts – they don't care about you and they only want to push you through further interviewing stages, so that they can end up getting their bonuses. So most of them won't mind giving you the number range, as long as it means you proceed further in the interviewing process. This way, you don't actually give the number yourself to the company and the recruiter takes care of it for you instead.

Leaving The Company To Decide On How Much You Should Get Payed

If you don't know the market value of the job position you're seeking, this is a fair strategy to use. I would also recommend trying this for someone who believes they are severely underpaid, even if someone else would suggest otherwise. I've successfully used this negotiation strategy when transitioning from one job to another and doubled my salary. During the interview rounds, I convinced I was very competent and enthusiastic about the company's job position. It did take a few times to persuade them I wasn't looking for a particular salary number and that I placed good faith in them for the offer they would make. To be fair, it was a well-known company and I did research their average salary ranges, but I couldn't trust that data enough to go for a number. Also, the salary I ended up with, had a higher ceiling than what the internet suggested for that position. The tricky part of this situation was that I was also a specialist, who was at the time severely underpaid, along with many other colleagues I worked with. To them, it looked like we were earning a fair amount and I even got ridiculed when I told them that I believe we could be earning much more.

However, your refusal to provide your expected salary can backfire on you and alienate your future employers. Which means you might be removed from the interviewing process. This is especially true for recruitment agencies, they are forced to work with an already defined salary ranges, so you can expect that they will not get off your back unless you do give them a number. Now with hiring managers, it's different, because if you go with this approach, they will end up offering you the lowest end of their defined salary range. To mitigate your chances of not getting the lowest end of an offer, always put emphasis, to no matter who you're speaking, that you trust that you BOTH understand the market value of the position, especially if you have already discussed the responsibilities of the role. On top of that you can reinforce your decision to not disclose the expected salary, by proving that you believe your main purpose for working inside the company is to seek growth opportunities. A lot of companies value employees, who seek long-term growth.

Providing Your Own Boosted Salary Range

One of the worst ways to start a negotiation is by providing your expected salary within a range. Doing this without a clear plan will end up as a pitfall for you. This almost always ends up with them coming back with a number that's in the lower end of the range. So if you ask for $40,000-$50,000, do not be surprised they come back with $39,000 - $41,000 - yes, you could give an even lower offer than the lowest one you asked for. It's in the company's best interest to capitalize on your inept negotiation skills. The only valid way to work with this range would be that you actually add a buffer on top of the range. Let's say 10% of what you earn right now and then use it as a starting point for your salary range. This way at least you end up with the lowest offer that is already 10% higher than your current salary.

Working With A Single Number

Preferred salary ranges are used all the time, but there are some challenges that come with them. First of all, you are never going to know, unless you have insider info, what the company is actually willing to pay the candidate. Second, sticking to a salary range can send a signal to the negotiator that you are not fully aware of the actual market value. If I don't trust myself enough to go with a salary range, I like to stick instead with a single number. I pick a number that would make me feel completely comfortable when starting my new job. If you give them a single number to work with, you are basically doing what is called "anchoring" them to negotiate. Anchoring in layman's terms means the first party who declares a number is the one who gains more leverage and flexibility at giving their own terms.

"Why Should We Pay You This Much?"

Sometimes you will be challenged to defend your preferred salary. There are a few ways to reason it. Drawing comparisons from the last jobs can help you to create stronger arguments. It might be because this job location is further from the one you're currently stationed at. It could be, you would be missing out on company benefits that you have at the current workplace. Make sure to always compare everything to your current job and in this way, answering the question to "Why" should become easier. It's also a valid tactic to reiterate the responsibilities you would be taking on and what skill set you would be bringing to the company. You need to connect the dots by saying that your skill X can be applied at their new position for solving task Y.

Conclusion

Negotiating for your salary can get tricky at times. There is no single winning method and often your success depends on which method of negotiation feels most natural to you. However, any type of negotiation you initiate is better than no negotiations. Any time a question for your expected salary comes up, try not to give it straight away and instead wait until the very end of the interviewing process. During negotiations, you might feel comfortable entrusting the company to decide the salary for you if you feel that you do not have a solid grasp on the job market. Your other options could be coming up with a single number and working from there or giving yourself a boosted salary range and at least know that the lowest end can still be a favorable increase for you. If asked to explain your reasoning for the salary, do not panic and instead come up with logical arguments, usually proving your point based on your skillset and competency.

BONUS THE MENTALITY OF A SUCCESSFUL JOB HUNTER

Over the years, I have learned, that my previous job experience, the skills I possess and the references I carry with me – none of that matters, if I do not enter the interview room with the right mentality. Your mentality can either set you up for a successful interview or create roadblocks that will make you look like a poor candidate for the job. Probably the most obvious of roadblocks that come from mentality as an example would be the "I am not good enough for this job" type of thinking. also known as Impostor's Syndrome. I have especially suffered from this roadblock for way too long, It is a nasty thing to carry around with you, and even to this day, it still finds a way to creep into my life. This or other negative thoughts and uncertainties in life is something you must learn to defeat. To do that, you will need to prepare yourself mentally for an interview. The goal of prepping yourself mentally is by coming to a realization, that you're the only one who knows the full story of your job experience and therefore, you are the only person who is best equipped at creating the most believable story about yourself. Telling this story will come with its own set of challenges. Here's how I have been prepping myself mentally and what sort of challenges I expect to encounter when I enter the interview room:

My Enthusiasm Is Key To Keeping The Conversation Lively

Excitement helps to escalate the awkwardness of interviewing into a more relaxed setting. To most people, talking about yourself is a vulnerable subject. The same applies to the interviewer, who may or may not be comfortable asking personal questions about you. To defuse tension in the room, I start by showing off I am enthusiastic about the job, when the introductory questions roll in (things like, "why do you want to work for us" or "how did you learn about the job" etc.). I always make it appear as if the question they've asked is very stimulating for me. You shouldn't answer every question this way, because then you end up looking disingenuous, but showing that you're listening and happy to answer is proof, that you can handle yourself in very personal situations.

If I Wasn't Good Enough For The Job, I Wouldn't Be Sitting In This Interview Room

They reached out to you. A meeting has been set-up. They are taking time out of their day to talk with you. Your resume was reviewed and they decided, you might have a future with them. All of this suggests you are now being considered for the position. Leave behind the doubt whether you're good enough and focus instead of figuring out how this company wants you to help them solve their problems.

I Am Instrumental, To The Jobs I Do

If a story you just told does not involve you as the centerpiece, then it's a story not worth telling. Any past accomplishments must be built around you – the person who made it happen. There's a notion that's going around that some people feel bad about themselves when they try to oversell what they do at their jobs. I personally think that a lot of things are overrated in life, such as superhero movies or owning an expensive set of steak knives. Heck, if you think about it, a lot of companies, when they put out their job listings, try to oversell on things as simple as office coffee machines. Or put meaningless fluff in their ads, such as "working with a creative and innovative team of people". Tell me you haven't seen that at least once in an ad. So put aside your modesty and when the time comes to tell them what you're currently working on, just be damn sure to convince them, that you're the hero of that story.

I Am Always Looking For Ways To Grow As A Professional

Whether the job requires you to flip burgers or draft legal documents, the key principle always remains the same – you need to learn and adapt to your new work environment. Interviewers are always looking for candidates who are willing to learn new things. What I like to do myself during an interview, is talk briefly about one of the optional job requirements that I do not possess, but already have spent time researching or practicing it. Usually, it's a low effort leg, but it shows them that I have spent some time figuring out the job requirements by myself. It never hurts and leaves the interviewer pleased with my curiosity.

I Am Interested In The Company And Its Business Model

No matter what position you're applying to, it's always important to show the interviewer, why the company excites you. When I was applying to a specialist position, that is exclusively technical and never gets exposed to the business side of the company, I took my time to talk about why I liked that company's business model. Afterwards, in later stages of interviewing, the hiring manager who interviewed, made a remark, that I left a strong impression for him because of my interest in the company's business side.

I Can Deal With Curveball Questions

When you start the meeting, it's important for you to begin as a calm and confident candidate. It just so happens, that quite often an interviewer, especially if its a technical one, will throw you what's known as a curveball question – something that usually has nothing to do with the job. Its main purpose is to catch you off-guard. Imagine if someone asks you what ice is made of. When you're calm and collected, you can laugh it off and even decline to answer it, because it's that obvious. But when you're in a high-stress situation, especially if that someone who is asking you appears to be more knowledgeable and intimidating, maybe even words the question differently, let's say asks you to "Tell me what are the main properties of ice" and you then start to panic, give away the answer reluctantly - "I think it's water, right?". You just made yourself appear weak and lose the confidence you previously entered with. If you can detect a curveball question being asked, your best bet is to laugh it off or act pleasantly insulted that you're getting asked something so simple or irrelevant. Sometimes, professionalism needs to be put aside and dominance has to enter the play. You need to show that you take yourself seriously as a professional. Now, if you cannot detect a curveball question, because you don't know an answer to it, you need to stay calm. Ask them to repeat the question. Put on your best, puzzled look you have and stare off into a distance like you're trying to understand the question itself. You can brush it off as an excuse for being hard to interpret. Everyone's mind works differently and if you've ever tried explaining something unusual, each person ends up with different comprehension. Same thing with interview questions – most of the things you get asked are easy to comprehend, but you can blame curveball questions for being intelligible.

I Answer Pervasive Questions In A Genuine Way

There will be questions that will try to poke at your weaknesses or past failures. You must avoid by all means providing crappy cookie-cutter answers such as "I am too hardworking" or "I wasn't able to attend my CEO's wedding". That last part might actually crack a smile. Still, when I get asked to talk about my failures, I am looking to tell a story, in which I can self-critique myself so that I can show I am self-aware of my shortcomings. These are my favorite questions to answer because you can get the interviewer to sympathize with you.

My Answers Are Concise And To The Point

Just because you've got invited for an interview, does not mean that the interviewer will give his full attention to you. These days, everyone's attention span has become much shorter, due to how technology has impacted our daily lives. Add the fact that you're not the first person to come for an interview, things you start saying will repeat themselves from other candidates. Learning to get your points across fast and simple is a key skill you must adopt for the interviewing mentality. If you're the type of person who likes to talk a lot, practice answering them by first writing down on paper and then removing words or even sentences that add little to no value to your answer. As an alternative, record yourself giving an answer, listen to the recording and make a new recording with an even shorter answer. Aim to answer even the most difficult of questions under a minute.

I Understand The Responsibilities Of The Offered Job

There will be a time when you will be juggling several job interviews. Part of the interviewer's job is figuring out how motivated you are for the position they're offering. You will need to keep yourself informed about each job you're applying to, to pass the motivation check. It's a big red flag for the interviewer if you have only a vague understanding of the job position and have no way of relating your existing skillset to it. Fear not, I understand that the biggest motivation for a job, quite often, is money. It also happens, that quite often, because HR or recruitment agencies themselves do not know exactly what the company is looking for, they create vague job descriptions. The easiest way of transitioning into understanding job requirements is by asking what the company is doing right now – what are their projects, how does their organizational structure look like, which department you would be working at, how many people in the department, whom you would be reporting to, who would be your teammates and so on. By asking these questions, you start to build an understanding of the company, its projects and the people work there. It becomes easier to pinpoint and understand the responsibilities of the job. Rule of thumb is to first ask as many questions as you can about the job, before proceeding to explain how you would be fit for the job. Always remember to research every word of the job listing that you're unfamiliar with. Try to find ways of relating your skills to the job requirements, before going into the interview. A combination of preparing before the interview and the on-site interview answers should net you a rough idea of what the hell the company actually wants you to do. The reality is that not every job is attractive. Companies tend to sugar coat, over-promise or straight up lie about what you'll be doing for them, just to entice you to come for work for them. Interviewers themselves know the position's turnover rate. Its often these are entry-level job positions, but candidates who've been working for years might not even be able to recognize what position they are applying to. The same can be reversed and it could be a high-level position, without the candidate realizing it. I personally believe that the biggest deal-breaker in an interview is the failure to comprehend the job position. Interviewers are not stupid – they can detect desperation and even worse – they can figure out your true motivation. They will come to a conclusion you're only here for the money if you're not asking enough questions about the job and the company. So when the interview is about to conclude and it's your time to do the final pitch, remember all the details you've gathered about the job and create a narrative of why you're the perfect candidate for the job.

Conclusion

The first interviews are always the hardest. Whether you're going to them after a long break or you're a fresh college student, interviewing itself is a skill that proves how well you sell yourself. And like any other skill, without constant practice, it will deteriorate over time. But learning how to sell yourself for the job is also the question of how motivated you are. The majority of our time, we feel uninspired and our life switches to autopilot. It can get really depressive when someone asks you to recall what you've done last week and you stumble to collect your memories. Most of our days are unexciting and the jobs we work, no matter how engaging they were at the beginning, have become as part of our routine. We get so self-absorbed in our own lives, that we forget how to tell our story to strangers. During an interview, you must get rid of monotony from your life and highlight key points of your career that you can use to craft a powerful message to the interviewer about yourself. I have found, that these key points for preparing yourself mentally should help you evoke your interviewing skills and set you on the right track.

EPILOGUE

The material you have read was based on the many interviews I have had over ten years and three different job sectors. I am sharing this material as someone who has been in the trenches and experienced everything there is to job hunting. You might be wondering, why would I, the author, change jobs so frequently? Was I really good at selling myself, but a terrible employee? Yes and sort of.

See, I strongly believe that the productiveness of the company is based on the Pareto Principle, also known as the 80/20 rule. This principle states, that 80% of the effects come from 20% of the causes. The same parallel can be drawn with the company's employees. I was never in the 20% and will never be there. To be that person, you must either be fluent in company politics or be in a position, where the job you do has control over the company's business. The 20% know how to distribute their time effectively and usually possess a very rare set of skills to solve many aching company problems. Some of the titles these people have are managers, subject matter experts, and contractors. Managers make decisions and receive recognition, subject matter experts solve real problems and contractors are the expensive versions of subject matter experts. The rest of the employees are there to keep the company afloat. It might sound grim, but that's what I have learned and contributes to one of the reasons why I hop around my jobs so often.

How it usually starts out, is I get into a honeymoon phase with my new job. Then, little by little, cracks would start showing up and you can't help but notice that each company has its own set of internal problems. The biggest trigger for me to start looking for a new job would be when layoffs start happening. There's a saying that everyone is replaceable... Unfortunately, I have witnessed that happening in my life far too many times and have developed a rather negative outlook because of it. Job hunting has turned into a business for the hiring sector because retaining employees is at an all-time low. It has become completely acceptable for you to change your job every few years.

Although everything I said so far sounds cynical, to me at least, this presents relief, when I am job hunting. If you set your expectations low, you can spend less time panicking during interviews and instead pose sharper questions for the interviewer. I never worry too much about myself or what I will say, I instead focus my efforts on examining how the interviewer behaves and what tidbits of crucial information they will give up. Just like people, no one is a saint and that applies to companies. Each of these companies has their problems and I can guarantee you, none of them will ever reveal them to you during the interview.

So I say this: take what you have learned from this

THE MENTALITY OF A SUCCESSFUL JOB HUNTER

book and see the results for yourself. The hiring sector likes to complicate job hunting, but the reality is that all you need is a primer, such as this book you just read. You have learned the essentials for demystifying job hunting. Most of the other candidates whom you will be competing against will be at a disadvantage because they did not bother learning the fundamentals. Without a solid foundation, they'll have trouble creating anything of value. They don't stand a chance against you. So go out there and stay sharp. You are now a job hunting pro.

ABOUT THE AUTHOR

Toby Tuckerman is the pen name used by a highly successful product manager in the tech industry.

Now in his late 30s, he has gained invaluable experience in both large corporate environments as well as small startup companies.

He has since then turned to entrepreneurship and decided to share his knowledge of job hunting, self-employment, online businesses and more.

In his first book Job Hunting Pro, he shares his step by step process on how to find a job. He has answered thousands of interview questions, wrote hundreds of resumes and managed to negotiate every salary successfully. He has figured out how recruitment works and knows how to present himself as the best candidate. He has also interviewed many candidates as a hiring manager.

Besides his professional career, Toby loves to travel around the world and spends months absorbing every country's culture as a digital nomad.

www.ingramcontent.com/pod-product-compliance
Lightning Source LLC
Chambersburg PA
CBHW051538240526
45465CB00027B/608